D1483969

LIVING in HOPE
of ETERNAL LIFE

LIVING in

of

HOPE
ETERNAL LIFE

An Exposition of the Book of Titus

By PAIGE PATTERSON

Foreword by Wayne E. Ward

ZONDERVAN PUBLISHING HOUSE

GRAND RAPIDS, MICHIGAN

Dedicated to

My Parents

HONEY and PATEE

(Dr. and Mrs. T. A. Patterson)
of Dallas, Texas, who taught
me early in life to love Jesus
and to trust His Word, the Bible

FOREWORD

One of the greatest needs of our day is serious study of the Bible and skillful application of its message to contemporary life and problems. This is literally *our only hope*. The philosophies of men are bankrupt — we have listened to the sound of our own voices and have found ourselves in confusion, violence, and despair. In the midst of all the "orgies of race and clan" we need the clear, ringing voice of divine truth to judge us and to guide us.

Most Christians will agree with this, but few are willing to pay the price in language study, historical investigation, and surrender to the Spirit's guidance — in order to bring the living message of the Bible directly into our lives today. But when deep and dedicated study of the Word of God is combined with practical experience in evangelism, in the pastoral ministry, and in encounter with the biting challenge of today's youth, it is an event worth noting.

This is such a book. It is written by a young man who can identify with the searching, questioning spirit of our day — for he is one of this generation. His book breathes the practical insight of daily witnessing for Christ — for, from his teen-age years, he has been remarkably effective as an evangelist. He demonstrates an unusual maturity because he has wrestled with all kinds of pastoral problems. Most significant of all, because of a gift for language and a deep interest in New Testament Greek, he has already spent all his college and seminary years in the intensive study of the Greek New Testament.

This exposition of *Titus* is the first published result of his labors. It is distinctive because it challenges some prevailing modern views of the Pastoral Epistles and, from a conservative viewpoint, opens up the meaning of the Greek text with a skill that must command the respect of anyone.

For those who believe that the Bible interpreter should be a deeply committed Christian — a skilled student of the biblical language — an experienced servant of Christ Jesus — and a firm believer in the authority of the Bible as the Word of God — this commentary will be a model. We need one on every book of the New Testament which will open up its message and apply it to our lives today in the same effective way!

WAYNE E. WARD

Southern Baptist Theological Seminary
Louisville, Kentucky

CONTENTS

Foreword

Preface

PREFACE

This exposition of the Epistle to Titus is intended to be used as parallel reading for a study of the book of Titus. The book is the result of a Bible study prepared and presented at the Southern Baptist Assembly, Glorieta, New Mexico, in the summer of 1966.

I gratefully acknowledge the tremendous help of Dr. Wayne E. Ward of Southern Baptist Theological Seminary, Dr. Clark H. Pinnock of New Orleans Baptist Theological Seminary, Dr. Samuel J. Mikolaski of New Orleans Baptist Theological Seminary, Dr. Malcolm Tolbert of New Orleans Baptist Theological Seminary, Dr. Theron V. Farris of the Evangelism Division of the Baptist General Convention of Texas, and Rev. Jerry Perrill, a fellow student at New Orleans Baptist Theological Seminary, for their helpful comments in regard to this book. The interpretations of this book are the author's and do not necessarily represent the feelings of these men. The translation of the Scripture passages has been made directly from the Greek New Testament text by the author. I further acknowledge the helpfulness of three grammarians who read the manuscript — Mrs. H. F. Weatherly, Mrs. Douglas Carter, and my wife Dorothy.

I am also grateful to my wife Dorothy and our daughter Mary Elizabeth for their patience and prayers during the preparation of this manuscript. Most of all I would express my appreciation to Dorothy for her encouragement and work on the book. Had it not been for her persistence, I probably would not have submitted this work for publication.

PAIGE PATTERSON

Chapter One

LIVING IN HOPE OF ETERNAL LIFE

An Introduction to Titus

The brief epistle addressed to Titus belongs to a group of three letters, including I and II Timothy, which have been designated, *The Pastoral Epistles*. Although neither Titus nor Timothy was actually a local pastor, the appellation appears to be a fair one, since all three letters deal with practical issues in the lives of individuals and local congregations. The message of Titus has sometimes been neglected, with more attention having been given to the longer books of the New Testament; or occasionally it has suffered lack of attention because of its similarity to the other two pastoral letters of Paul. Nevertheless, the message of Titus is distinctive and fresh. It gives a picture of how twice-born men ought to live in the present age; and it provides a reason for living in separation to God — namely, the promised appearing of Christ. Furthermore, its account of what actually transpires in salvation is as clear an analysis as can be found in the New Testament. We would not be wrong to consider the Epistle to Titus as the Christian's handbook for last-day living.

Authorship and Date

The first verse of our letter identifies Paul as the author. It has been popular for some theologians systematically to question the apostolic authorship of various New Testament books. The Pastoral Epistles have not escaped such efforts. The Pauline authorship has been subject to continual attack.[1] It is not in the scope of this commentary to deal exhaustively with this charge, since it has been adequately treated elsewhere.[2] Suffice it to say that one of the major reasons for questioning Pauline authorship is that of a vocabulary difference between Paul's longer letters and the Pastoral Epistles. Let it be sufficient to echo what numerous believing scholars who love God's Word have already stated, that is: if Shakespeare or Milton were subject to such careful vocabulary analysis, one could easily claim that much of their writing was in reality pseudonymous.

[1]For example: C. K. Barrett, *The Pastoral Epistles in the New English Bible* (Oxford: Clarendon Press, 1963), or P. N. Harrison, *The Problem of the Pastorals* (Oxford: University Press, 1921).

[2]William Hendriksen, "Exposition of the *Pastoral Epistles*," *New Testament Commentary* (Grand Rapids: Baker Book House, 1957).

Note also that those who question the Pauline authorship of the Pastoral Epistles do not base their views on any textual problem in regard to the appearance of Paul's name in the text as author. Consequently, it may be seen that to maintain non-Pauline authorship it is necessary to approach these Epistles from a rather skeptical position, which is certainly not becoming to those dealing with God's revelation. Could it be that Titus and Timothy speak so loudly to contemporary theology that its advocates desire to react to their message like the proverbial ostrich and refuse to see the truth? Does it attempt to silence these sermons by removing apostolic authorship?

In faith, then, with excellent demonstrable evidence to authenticate our position, we accept the text as truthful in claiming Paul as its author. The great missionary evangelist, unmatched as a theologian, the apostle of our Lord, and the author of a large portion of our New Testament has presented to Christians of the twentieth century a guidebook for living in the last days.

The date of the Epistle is an open question. It appears to hinge on the question of whether Paul had one or two Roman imprisonments. I have accepted the date of A.D. 63 as serviceable on the basis of the following factors: (1) the optimistic ending of Luke's history in Acts, (2) a persistent tradition regarding further missionary journeys of Paul which were not recorded for us, and (3) other historical data of minor significance. This would necessitate Paul's release from prison at a point sometime after the close of Acts. This, of course, cannot be proven but nevertheless seems highly probable.[3] Following his release, Paul visited Crete and Spain, together with other places, finally arriving back in Rome, where he wrote II Timothy from prison. All had deserted him except Luke (II Timothy 4:11). Here, probably during his second imprisonment, he sealed his witness for Jesus in martyrdom.

Titus

Our epistle is addressed to Titus. The brief picture which we view of Titus in the New Testament is a happy one. His name is mentioned thirteen times in the New Testament. Because of this relatively brief mention he has not been given the consideration which he deserves. Titus was a Greek who, according to Paul, was a convert of his (Titus 1:4). His importance in the early church can be assessed in at least two respects. (1) Paul took him to the Jerusalem Conference according to Galatians 2:1-3. Hendriksen has suggested that Titus was employed as a test case to prove to the conference that Gentiles could be heirs of salvation without submitting to Jewish circumcision.[4]

---

[3]For an excellent discussion of the last days of Paul's life (as they possibly occurred), see Hendriksen, *Ibid.*, pp. 39-44.

[4]*Ibid.*, p. 37.

(2) Evidently Titus was so effective in his ministry that Paul developed great confidence in him. When there was trouble in the church at Corinth, Titus was the apostolic messenger to the church. So effective was Titus at Corinth that he was able to accomplish that which the great apostle himself had not managed to do. When the churches on the isle of Crete suffered from doctrinal impurity and moral decay, once again, Titus was commissioned to rectify the situation. Indeed, an interesting relationship seems to suggest itself in the New Testament. Whereas Paul was actually closer to Timothy, his beloved son in the faith, he was evidently conscious that this young man Titus really possessed greater ability and determination. This is not meant to underestimate the character or service of Timothy. It is rather to affirm that Titus was a young man not only of great tact but also of unyielding conviction and forceful determination.

It is to Titus, Paul's young protege, therefore, that the epistle is addressed. He had been left on the island of Crete for the purpose of guiding the infant churches in their labor for the Master.

The Island of Crete

Crete (modern Candia) is one of the larger Mediterranean islands, bordering the Aegean Sea. It is approximately 156 miles long, and its width ranges from 7 to 30 miles. The island in ancient times was dotted from one end to the other with cities such as Cnossus, Paistos, Haga Triada, and Fair Havens. A mountain range stretches the length of the island, reaching a maximum height of 8,193 feet in the now famous Mt. Ida. We are indebted to Sir Arthur Evans for major archaeological work on the island.

Crete is no mean island in ancient history. It is rich not only in legend but also in its relation to Greek history in general. To begin with, Mt. Ida is the traditional birthplace of Zeus. Zeus had a brilliant son, according to Greek myth, named Minos, who became king of the island. That one named Minos was once a powerful king on the island appears to be well substantiated. Most of the Greeks considered Minos a superb ruler, but the Athenians, who evidently were treated harshly by Minos, had little appreciation for him.

Minos wedded Pasiphae, the daughter of the Sun, and with that event we are back to legend. Minos was religious by nature; and being dependent upon the sea, he had great reverence for Poseidon, god of the sea. Poseidon, in return for this favoritism, sent to Minos a beautiful white bull to be sacrificed in the god's honor. So beautiful was the animal that Minos blundered by retaining the white bull and sacrificing an inferior victim. This so angered Poseidon that he caused Pasiphae to develop a tragic lust for the bull. Disguised as a cow, she satisfied her hideous passion and gave birth to Minotaur, who was a fearful monster — half bull and half man. Minos shut this monster up in Labyrinth, and legend strongly affirms that he thereafter exacted human tribute as food for his half-bull monster.[5]

As a result of these ancient legends, an extensive "bull lore" was developed on the island of Crete. It may be seen that with such a grotesque story in the background of this island, the inhabitants, known as Minoans (after Minos), naturally fell into a rather low standard of morality. This problem was acutely present when Paul wrote to Titus (Titus 1:12).

Titus was thrust into such an atmosphere as this with the responsibility of correcting the problems in the local churches on Crete. Little is known of the origin of Christianity on the island. Paul was there briefly at Fair Havens on his journey to Rome as a prisoner. Whether or not Paul was responsible for the earliest Christian witness on Crete is impossible to tell. It is obvious that he had a close fellowship with the churches there. After having visited the churches himself, he departed, leaving Titus in charge as an apostolic delegate. As will be observed later, Titus had a mammoth task. Not only did the churches find themselves in the midst of gross immorality, but also the Judaizers had already arrived with all their legalistic additions to the faith.

Purpose of the Epistle

Several purposes for the writing of this epistle are evident in the letter. (1) Titus was reminded of his responsibility to see that each congregation of believers had a qualified pastor. (2) He was to be insistent upon sound doctrine. (3) He was to instruct the people in the art of Christian living in a pagan environment. (4) He was to go to Paul as soon as possible, taking with him others needed by the apostle.

With this brief background, we shall now direct our attention to an exposition of the letter to Titus.

---

[5]J. R. Rose, *A Handbook of Greek Mythology* (New York: E. P. Dutton & Company, Inc., n. d.), p. 182 ff.

Chapter Two

IN HOPE OF ETERNAL LIFE

Titus 1:1-5

1 Paul a bond servant of God, and an apostle of Jesus Christ with reference to the faith of the elect of God and to a full knowledge of the truth which is according to godliness,
2 Upon hope of life eternal which the God who cannot lie promised before the times of the ages,
3 But revealed in his own time his word by preaching with which I was entrusted according to the decree of our Saviour God,
4 To Titus a genuine child according to a common faith; grace and peace from God the Father and Christ Jesus our Saviour.
5 For this cause I left you in Crete in order that you might correct the things which are lacking and appoint elders in each city as I commanded you.

Verse 1 *Paul a bond servant of God, and an apostle of Jesus Christ with reference to the faith of the elect of God and to a full knowledge of the truth which is according to godliness,*

The epistle to Titus begins with the salutation of Paul. Paul identifies himself by expressing two relationships which he maintained toward God. The first of these relationships is one of which every believer ought to partake, while the other is an office which only a select few were privileged to hold. Paul is first of all a bond servant of God. The Greek word *doulos* is frequently used with reference to one who was born into slavery. It is significant that every man who desires to submit to the service of the Christ must be brought into that service through the second or spiritual birth. Also it is essential that Christians today begin to understand themselves to be committed bond servants of Christ. We are not our own. We have put our hands to the plow, and we cannot look back. We have crucified the old man. We have died to ourselves in order that we may live to Christ. This means that like the great Paul our finest effort must be used to ascertain the will of Christ. And, having ascertained that will, one should press toward the mark of the high calling of God with diligence.

But Paul is not only a slave for God; he also occupies the esteemed position of an apostle of the Lord Jesus Christ. Some of the factors which were necessary for apostleship were: (1) The apostles had been chosen, called, and sent forth by Christ Himself. (2) They were eye witnesses to His resurrection. (3) They were endowed with a special measure of the Holy Spirit. (4) Their office was not restricted to a local church, and it was a life-time office. So Paul writes as both a willing servant of God and as an appointed apostle of Jesus Christ.

He is writing to Titus with regard to the faith of the elect of God and the full knowledge of truth.[1] The phrase, *the elect of God,* has reference to believers and must be understood in the light of I Peter 1:2, which declares that election took place according to God's foreknowledge. The faith of the elect is the subject of particular interest since the shaking winds of doctrinal instability had already begun to ravage the churches on Crete. Paul desired that amid such circumstances, the followers of Jesus might have full knowledge of the truth which is according to godliness. The a.v. translates *epignosin* as *acknowledging.* However, this term makes use of the word *knowledge* coupled with the Greek preposition *epi,* meaning *upon,* to indicate *knowing thoroughly* or *having full knowledge.* The use of the preposition expresses a greater participation by the knower in the object known.

If the Christians on the island of Crete are to be able to offer an adequate defense for their faith, their knowledge of truth must be as complete as possible this side of heaven. The very first verse of this epistle speaks to the church today. Membership rolls are more extensive than ever, but godlessness more nearly characterizes many modern Christians than does the godliness about which Paul spoke. Evangelism is often left to the pastor and the missionary. The concept of a church with a ministry appears old-fashioned in some quarters. Could the reason for this be that individual believers do not possess a full knowledge of the truth which is according to godliness?

It is difficult to ascertain whether the Bible has suffered most at the hands of so called "theologians" or just from the shallow study habits of individual believers. In any case, it is not really the Word of God which has suffered but rather the masses of Christian people who have tried to play the game of life without knowing the rule book.

The answer to the problem of declining spirituality and limited impact on our world is the reactivation of the individual believer-priest. Bible study must not be left to the theologian nor evangelism to the pastor. The man who would lift a great weight cannot do so using both arms and only one leg, while the other leg remains relaxed and inactive. Both legs are necessary for strength and balance. If the body of Christ influences this world, it will be as a balanced unit of personal witness resulting from individual Bible study and prayer.

---

[1]The Greek preposition *kata* has been here translated *with reference to.* This is one of its rarer meanings but is more acceptable at this point than the usual *according to.*

Verse 2 *Upon hope of life eternal which the God who cannot lie promised before the times of the ages,*

Even as Paul is writing, he is standing securely upon a rock of hope, the hope of eternal life. The A.V. translates the phrase, *in hope of eternal life*. Literally, however, it should be *upon hope of eternal life*. Everything that Paul believes or does is built upon that hope of eternal life. And the use of the term, *hope*, is not meant to imply any doubt as to the certainty of its fulfillment. The early Christian understood that his hope was not in some remote possibility but was grounded in God who cannot lie. Jesus said, "Whosoever heareth my word, and believeth on him that sent me, hath everlasting life . . . ."

This is a promise which cannot be broken. The Christian hope is a sure thing. It is based on an earnest expectation of the future. It means that there is a unique trust in God. And it enables us to wait patiently in an antagonistic world for the consummation of our salvation.[2] In other words, our hope is as sure as our trust in Jesus for salvation. The child of God need not fear at all. This hope is based on the promise of a God who cannot lie — a promise which was made before the times of the ages.

The closing phrase of verse two and the opening words of verse three combine in the original language of the New Testament to present the reader with an interesting contrast. A word meaning *time* is used in both verses, but in each verse it is a different Greek word. Verse two tells of the hope of eternal life promised by God before the times, *kronos*, of the ages. Verse three begins by announcing that God revealed Himself in His own time, *Kairos*. Often in the New Testament these two words seem to be used interchangeably. In this instance, however, there appears to be a deliberate altering of the word choice in verse three. The sense of the passage becomes exciting if this be true. God promised eternal life in Christ before time as man reckons it *(kronos)* ever began. But in His own choice of time *(kairos)* He revealed Himself in Christ. *Kronos* seems to be time as man understands time. *Kairos* is contrasted with it and reveals how God looks at time.

Galatians 4:4 records that *in the fullness of time (kronos), God sent forth his son.* But here the viewpoint is different. When the history of mankind had reached the proper point, Christ was sent into the world. But as far as God was concerned it took place in His own time *(kairos)*. Perhaps this will help us to understand how Christ could

---

[2]See article on "Hope," Gerhard Kittel, ed., *Theological Dictionary of the New Testament*, Vol. II.

Verse 3 *But revealed in his own time his word by preaching with which I was entrusted according to the decree of our Saviour God,*

have been slain before the foundation of the world as John declares in Revelation 13:8. As men count time, Christ was crucified on a given date in *kronos* time. But with God, whose *kairos* time is distinct, the Lamb had already been slain before the world began. This is why the blood of Christ was efficacious for Old Testament believers living prior to the time of the incarnation. As far as God was concerned, the sacrifice of Jesus was a certainty, and the Lamb's blood covered the sins of Abraham, Isaac, Joseph, and others.

What was it, though, that was revealed in God's own time? It was the Word of God which came in its final form as a result of the life, death, and resurrection of Jesus. And, it was revealed in a most unusual manner. The vehicle of revelation was a strange gift called preaching. It was a gift which was entrusted to Paul according to the express command of his Saviour God. Several things are worthy of consideration in this verse. First, Paul considered the Word of God to be a precious treasure with which God had entrusted him. The force of this word *entrusted* (A.V. *committed*) may be observed by noting that it is the same word used for that essential factor in salvation — *trusting* Christ. The Word of God was committed to Paul as a sacred trust. Small wonder that with such a treasure he should traverse large segments of the world to share its wealth. Is it not to be expected that Paul would be willing to die at any moment in the defense of his treasure? And can we demand any less of ourselves than we do of this apostle?

Another item of interest is that Paul had been given this treasure and his preaching commission according to the express command of God. Occasionally one meets those who do not advocate a God-called ministry, and one is forced to wonder if they have ever read much from Paul's pen. His mission was one for which he had been expressly commissioned.

Verse 4 *To Titus a genuine child according to a common faith; grace and peace from God the Father and Christ Jesus our Saviour.*

Having thus introduced himself, Paul identifies the one for whom the letter is intended. It is addressed to Titus, who is said to be the *genuine* or *legitimate child* of Paul *according to a common faith.* The *common faith,* is, of course, a mutual trust in Christ. Titus is his child in the faith in that Paul was the one who led him to Jesus. Moreover, there was no hypocrisy in the faith of Titus. He was a *genuine child* in the faith. He had proved to the world that the regeneration of the Holy Spirit had changed and redirected his whole life. The *common faith* is probably more than just that faith in Christ. This saving faith forms the basis for the whole body of Christian truth and teaching. This Christian teaching was also shared by Titus.

Paul continues by pronouncing *grace and peace* upon Titus. The word *mercy* is not part of most of the better texts.[3] Whether included or excluded, no violence is done to the message of the text. The order of the terms is correct. There can be no *peace* until there has first of all been *grace*. Most of the unsaved world is in a mad dash to try to chase down peace. How little do they realize that it comes not by running but by praying, "God, be merciful to me a sinner." Peace is a gift and an assurance that follows the work of God's grace in the heart of any penitent, trusting individual. These gifts of grace and peace come not from Paul. They are from God the Father and Christ Jesus the Saviour. Let it never be forgotten that no priest or any other human being can bestow these gifts. They are uniquely the gifts of God.

In his commentary on Ephesians, the late Dr. H. A. Ironside has brought to our attention an occurrence in the opening passage of that book which takes place here also.[4] It is common for most of the writers of the New Testament to speak of the Lord as Jesus Christ, but Paul often refers to Him as *Christ Jesus*. The disciples first knew this God-man as Jesus and only later, perhaps at Caesarea-Philippi, understood Him to be the Christ, the anointed one or Messiah. But Paul met Him for the first time on the Damascus Road, and he met Him there not as the man Jesus but as the risen and glorified Christ. Thus, Paul not only knew Him as Saviour but also had an abiding vision of Jesus as the Christ of God.

Verse 5 *For this cause I left you in Crete in order that you might correct the things which are lacking and appoint elders in each city as I commanded you.*

After completing his salutation the great apostle reminds Titus of his mission on Crete. He was left there that the things which were wanting might be set in order. Paul's visit to Crete was probably of short duration. He needed to go elsewhere, and Titus was left with instructions to set in order those things in the churches that were in need of trained attention. The word *epidiorthoō* employed at this point is of interest. It was sometimes used by medical writers con-

---

[3]The various texts offer an assortment of readings at this point. Abundant are the sources which include *mercy;* but the reliability of those which do not have it, such as Sinaiticus, is sufficient to justify its exclusion from the text.

[4]H. A. Ironside, *In the Heavenlies* (New York: Loizeaux Brothers, Inc., 1957), p. 12.

cerning the setting of broken limbs. It is possible that Paul uses medical terminology in this instance to link this reminder to his discussion of healthy teachings in verse nine. In any case, there was obvious confusion in some of the churches on Crete of both a doctrinal and moral nature. Titus was to correct these problems.

The second part of his task was to appoint in each city elders or pastors, as Paul had instructed him. These were not to be the random choice of Titus but rather the choice of God with Titus acting as God's agent in appointing them for service in local congregations.

The word *elders* is used in two different respects in the book of Titus. It denotes elderly men in the church in chapter two. It is used here to refer to the bishop, overseer, or pastor of these churches. The word does not refer to deacons in the New Testament, but rather to the bishops or pastors of the churches.

Note that the term is plural. Most of these early churches had a plurality of pastors. In all probability they each supervised and led in some particular ministry of the church. This New Testament pattern, which has to some degree been abandoned, needs to be given a careful look by our churches today which would model themselves after those early assemblies. Titus was to lead these churches in finding and then appointing God's minister for each of the congregations on the isle of Crete. This was no small responsibility for such a young man.

Chapter Three

PATTERNS FOR PREACHERS

Titus 1:6-9

6 If any be irreproachable, the husband of one wife, having children who are believers, who are not accused of reckless abandon or disorderliness.

7 For the bishop must be irreproachable as a steward of God, not self-willed, not easily angered, not given to wine, not one of violence, not eager for gain,

8 But he must be a lover of strangers and a lover of good, having a sound mind, just, holy, self-controlled,

9 Holding firmly to the teaching of the faithful word, in order that he may be able by healthy doctrine both to persuade and to refute the ones who are speaking against healthy doctrine.

Verses six through nine of this first chapter establish something of a ministerial standard or, as we have suggested in our chapter heading, a pattern for preachers. Such listings as this one and similar ones in Timothy are frequently employed in ordination services, but the continuing importance of these patterns must also be considered. Some, who are not preachers, will doubtless wonder how this list of ministerial prerequisites concerns them. In answer it should be noted that there are several areas in which this brief passage should serve as a valuable guide for both preachers and laymen.

First, these verses certainly serve as a pattern for preachers. The one who would know the high demands of Christ upon those who preach His Word need look no further than Titus 1:6-9. If God calls a man to the ministry, this man must be willing to conform to the Spirit-breathed requirements for the ministry. But this list does not cease to be important after ordination. Whether a man is in a large pastorate, a thriving mission work, or even a ministry of teaching others, these are still God's commands. How different would the attitudes of many of God's chosen vessels be were they to examine regularly their own lives and ministries in the light of this pattern. Such submission to God's spiritual scrutiny would certainly result in a new humility on the part of the preacher. Along with that humility would come a new dependence upon the power and grace of God. It is this last factor that equips a man for a great ministry.

But there is also benefit here for the layman. First, every layman ought to be aware of what he is to expect of his pastor or of any preacher. All of the problems which develop in a local church are not "preacher problems," but some are. When there is a problem with one of God's men, it may be traced often to the neglect of one of the essentials listed by Paul in Titus 1. Every believer has a right to expect his pastor to measure up to the pattern described in Titus. And a dedicated pastor will want his flock to expect this of him.

Second, Paul told Timothy to let no man despise his youth but to be an example to the believers. In other words, Paul was instructing Timothy to arrange his life so that it would be worthy of imitation by the saints in the churches. These requirements listed in Titus would be of the same importance. When considered in this perspective, these are worthy goals for the layman as well as the preacher. With these thoughts in mind, consider carefully the text. Titus has been reminded of his instructions for promoting Christian missions on Crete. Elders or pastors were needed in the churches. Those whom Titus appointed were to meet the following qualifications:

Verse 6 *If any be irreproachable, the husband of one wife, having children who are believers, who are not accused of reckless abandon or disorderliness.*

Elders as pastors were to be irreproachable or blameless. The word used is *anegklētos*. It is a compound form made up of *a*, which is called an alpha privative and negates the word which immediately follows it, and *egkaleō* meaning *to accuse*. Thus the meaning literally is *non-chargeable*, and hence blameless or irreproachable. There are always some who will try to disparage a good name, but in the final analysis the preacher should stand above accusation. Actually Paul uses this word in two senses. Here it doubtless refers to moral and ethical uprightness of character. In I Corinthians 1:8 Paul says, "Who shall also confirm you unto the end, that ye may be blameless in the day of our Lord Jesus Christ." Here the term is used of the Christians standing before their God. The coming of Christ is in view, and it is said that the believer will be blameless before Christ. No accusation can be brought against him because he stands clothed, not in his own righteousness, but in the righteousness of Christ. In both senses the bishop or pastor must be blameless. He must have had a life-changing encounter with Christ, and he must continue living above reproach if he is to be effective for Christ.

Nothing can be more detrimental to the work of a pastor than family turmoil. Therefore, the apostle next gives some instructions concerning the family of the preacher. The pastor is to be the husband of one wife. This, of course, does not eliminate the unmarried man from the ministry. The thought is rather that he must not have more than one wife.

It is a standing joke that "preachers' kids" are the meanest kids anywhere. The facts hardly bear this out, but there are some restrictions regarding the children of the pastor. They are to be believers. The a.v. reads *faithful children,* but the sense is really *children of the faith.* If a man cannot lead his own children to Jesus at a tender age, whom can he lead to Christ? The preacher ought never to be so busy that the salvation of his own children is neglected.

In addition to being believers, the pastor's children should conduct themselves in such a manner that they could not be accused of *reckless abandon* or of *disorderliness.* The word which I have translated *reckless abandon, asotia,* is the same word used in Luke 15:13 as descriptive of the prodigal son when it is said that "he spent his substance in riotous living." This word originally meant *incurable,* and thus one who by the very manner of his life was destroying himself. The word does not signify extravagant living so much as it does wild, unconcerned living. Neither must the children of a pastor be accused of *disorderliness.* Actually this second word, *anupotakta,* seems to have to do with one's attitude toward constituted authority. Those who characteristically live a wild and unruly life are also usually insubordinate. Perhaps the best translation at this point would be, "not accused of insubordination." If one does not honor his parents and bow before proper authority, he is not likely to honor God nor willfully submit to His rule.

Verse 7 *For the bishop must be irreproachable as a steward of God, nor self-willed, not easily angered, not given to wine, not one of violence, not eager for gain.*

The bishop[1] himself must be blameless as a steward of God. He must not be self-willed. The word is *authade* which is a compound making use of the personal pronoun, *he,* and the Greek verb *hedomai* meaning *to enjoy one's self.* Thus a bishop is to guard himself against being a self-pleaser. It is far more important to be a God-pleaser.

A further requirement is that a bishop not be easily angered. If a man is not possessed of the Spirit of Christ, there are many things in the ministry which could easily provoke him to anger. And it would even be conceded that there are those occasions when a degree of righteous indignation is in order. However, it is never a Christ-like attitude to harbor wrath or anger nor to be easily driven toward it.

---

[1]The reader has doubtless noticed that we have used the terms bishop, elder, and pastor interchangeably. *Presbuteros,* meaning *elder,* and *episcopas,* meaning *bishop* (literally *overseer*), both designate the same New Testament officer, the pastor. The meaning of the term *bishop* has altered with the passing of the years. In the New Testament, the *bishop* was simply a local pastor. For an excellent discussion of this, see A. H. Strong, *Systematic Theology,* pp. 914 ff.

Nor should the preacher be given to wine. Not only is it imperative that the preacher abstain from strong drink altogether, but in this day in which the liquor industry grips modern society with such violent tenacity, the preacher ought to take his stand firmly against the use and sale of beverage alcohol.

Closely corresponding to the minister's command not to be easily angered is the command not to be given to violence, or as the A.V. puts it, *not a striker*. The Bible never records an incident in which a follower of Jesus struck an individual in anger except when Peter forcefully amputated the ear of Malchus. This brought only rebuke from the Master. Jesus is the Prince of Peace. Although the righteousness of God demands the punishment of the sinner who refuses the gift of God, the essential nature of God is still love, and He is preeminently a God of peace. The testimony of Stephen did not make such an impact on Paul because that deacon died fighting but rather because he died praying for his murderers. Jesus said, "If a man smites thee on one cheek, turn to him the other also." And John said, "Hereby we do know that we know him if we keep his commandments." As a unit the Bible forbids the Christian to allow anger to move him to violence.

The last of these negative commands forbids the man of God to be eager for material gain. If the Christian is *in but not of the world,* and if his heart is where his treasure is and his treasure is Jesus, then there is no need for material gain to be a goal of life. This does not mean that the minister or any Christian has an excuse to be careless in financial affairs or to fail to provide adequately for his family. Neither does it give a church the right to keep the minister on a starvation wage since he is not to be eager for gain. Paul reminds us in I Corinthians 9:9 that we are not to muzzle the ox while he works in the corn. Neither should a congregation fail to supply the needs of a hardworking, Spirit-led pastor. However, there is a subtle danger that lurks in the very heart of our materialistically-minded society. The desire for "things" is often a greater pressure than the desire for money itself. But the whole point of this last negative command is for the minister to guard himself carefully against becoming so addicted to any worldly material that he should lose sight of the more important treasure reserved in Heaven for all who trust in Jesus.

Verse 8 *But he must be a lover of strangers and a lover of good, having a sound mind, just, holy, self-controlled,*

The negative commands have been issued. Now there are some positive qualifications for the minister. First, he is to *be a lover of strangers.* This phrase is actually only one word in Greek and is of great interest. It is *philoxenon* from *phileō*, meaning *to love* or *to delight in* and *xenos*, meaning *strange, foreign,* or *alien.* Thus it might be translated, *one who delights in strangers.* It is a word that is used only rarely in the New Testament. However, there are at least two very good reasons for this command. First, the early Christians were very dependent upon one another for traveling accommodations. Not wishing to stay in the inns, travelers would seek a Christian home; and the result was often a wonderful fellowship together. It is to be feared that something of the joyousness of early Christian fellowship departed through the back door of the church as popularity walked in the front door. Jesus said, *"By this shall all men know that ye are my disciples if you have love one for the other."* It is a commentary on our love for Jesus and on how much we glory in His fellowship whenever we do not enjoy the presence of fellow-believers.

Second, if one takes it upon himself to befriend a stranger, the chances are that he will also have an opportunity to witness for the Lord. The coming of the apartment building, the practice of hiding behind denominational labels, and the natural distrust of others, which have become a part of the contemporary scene, have all combined to make witnessing more difficult. But a love for strangers and a sweet hospitality will melt many a hard heart and open the door for Jesus.

The preacher must also be *a lover of good.* The a.v. says *good men.* Although the word *men* does not actually occur in the text, the rendering is acceptable. It includes more than just *men,* though. It means that he is to be *a lover of good* in general. The preacher must likewise be of *a sound mind.* Intellectual attainment and spiritual prowess are not in opposition to one another. In fact, they are complementary.

Three other qualities are essential for the man of God. The first is that he be *just.* In relation to God man is *just* only when he has been reconciled to God through the blood of the Lord Jesus. In relation to his fellow man this is a command to uprightness in all his dealings, whether business or otherwise. Second, the minister is to be *holy.* This is not the usual word for *holy* in the New Testament. Barclay has defined this word *hosion* as *reverencing the fundamental decencies of life, the things which go back beyond any man-made law or regulation.*[2] Third, a bishop should be self-controlled. The word translated by the a.v. as *temperate* actually means *to be master of oneself.* For the Christian this self-control is really a self-mastery that enables one to place himself under the mastery of the Holy Spirit. If a man is mastered by anything else, he cannot be the servant of the Spirit.

[2]William Barclay, *The Letters to Timothy, Titus and Philemon* (Philadelphia: Westminster Press, 1960), p. 273.

The Lord requires that the servant of God yield his life to the mastery of the Spirit of God.

Verse 9 *Holding firmly to the teaching of the faithful word, in order that he may be able by healthy doctrine both to persuade and to refute the ones who are speaking against healthy doctrine.*

The importance of this last exhortation in verse nine could scarcely be overestimated. The preacher, and every other believer, should hold firmly to those teachings of the faithful Word. The word *antexomenon* has been translated *holding firmly.* This is one of the most picturesque words in Titus. It comes from two words, *anti,* meaning *against* and *ekō,* meaning *to have.* Thus literally it means *to have against.* In college days I remember watching two male social clubs engaged in a tug-of-war over a huge puddle of waist-deep, fresh mud. That particular location was chosen so that the losing team would not be difficult to identify when the tug-of-war was over. Well, one group prevailed, and the other group felt worse than Naaman emerging for the sixth time from the muddy waters of the Jordan. The group that prevailed avoided a muddy bath because they held the rope even against great odds. That is a little of the picture that is painted by this word. No matter what the obstacles may be and no matter who tries to take away the heart of the saving Gospel, the Christian is to hold on firmly to the teachings of the faithful Word. What are these teachings? They are God's revelation as recorded in the Scriptures.

There is a reason for holding firmly to the Word of God. The man of God must be able by sound doctrine both to persuade and to refute any who would speak against the way of the Lord. The words which the A.V. translates *sound doctrine* may be more literally translated as *healthy teachings.* The word *teachings* doubtless refers to the body of Old Testament Scripture along with the words of Jesus and the apostles, which eventually became the New Testament canon. The word *healthy* is from *hugiainousē,* which is a medical term often used to describe one who is the picture of health. Paul, John, Peter, and others recognized early the danger of unhealthy teachings. So dangerous did they consider false doctrine that Paul could write, "If an angel from heaven preach any other doctrine, let him be accursed." These apostles realized that wrong doctrine would be disastrous with the eternal consequence of hell for those who were led astray.

Armed with this healthy doctrine, the Christian pastor would be ready to refute that which was contrary to healthy doctrine and having refuted it to persuade those who were under its spell to submit to the claims of Christ. Verses seven and eight enumerate moral and ethical principles and attitudes which, if followed, will enable the minister to carry out effectively his commission as given in verse nine.

Chapter Four
CLOSING THE MOUTHS OF LIONS

Titus 1:10-16

10 For there are many insubordinate men who are vain talkers and deceivers, especially those of the circumcision,

11 Who must be silenced, who corrupt whole households teaching what they ought not for the sake of dishonest gain.

12 One of them, their own prophet said, Cretians are always liars, evil beasts, unemployed stomachs.

13 This witness is true. Because of this, rebuke them sharply in order that they may be healthy in the faith,

14 Not assenting to Jewish myths and commandments of men which pervert the truth.

15 To the pure all things are pure, but to those who are corrupt and unbelieving nothing is clean but even their minds and moral judgments are defiled.

16 They profess to know God, but in works deny him, being abominable and unbelieving and to every good work worthless.

The church of the Lord Jesus has suffered the heavy hand of persecution from its inception to the present day almost without interruption. It has had much of its history written in the blood of faithful witnesses. Ample opportunity has been given to practice the instructions of Jesus to *Pray for them that despitefully use you.* But the ministry of the church seems to have been affected far more by the subtlety of doctrinal error than by all of the physical torture that God's enemies could heap upon the heads of Christians.

Doctrinal difficulties have plagued the growth of the church in countless ways. From emotional excesses arising from a misunderstanding of the work of the Holy Spirit to pseudo-intellectualism resulting usually in a glorified humanism, denying the power of God, the church has been assailed by perverted doctrine.

Through such teaching the ugly gates of hades have lifted themselves against the body of Christ. It is comforting to remember the promise of the Master that these gates of hades will not overcome the church. Nevertheless, the church must be aware of Satan's assaults and answer them with the Word of God. This does not mean that the church is to become a group of theological detectives responsible for nothing but hunting down those who teach the doctrines of men as the commandments of God. However, as Vance Havner has well said, "The Church has a right to screen out the bugs while it lets in the light." [1] Therefore, Paul instructed Titus to choose only those who were healthy in doctrine to pastor the churches on Crete. Verses ten through sixteen explain why Titus must exercise such great care in this task.

Verse 10 *For there are many insubordinate men who are vain talkers and deceivers, especially those of the circumcision.*

Titus was to choose only those who were sound in doctrine because there were many insubordinate men who were vain talkers and deceivers, especially some of the legalistic Jews. The question then arises: Concerning what were these people insubordinate? The answer is that they were refusing to submit themselves to the authority of God's Word as revealed in the Old Testament and the words of Jesus and those with apostolic authority. Thus they were refusing the very rule of God. They were good talkers. They talked a great program for God's glory, but it was impossible to find anyone that had been brought to Jesus by these men. They believed themselves to be accomplished theologians, but their doctrines proved to be degrading and fruitless. Instead of evangels of God's pure Word, they were found to be deceivers not only of men's minds but also of their own minds.

Verse 11 *Who must be silenced, who corrupt whole households teaching what they ought not for the sake of dishonest gain.*

Paul demands that these deceivers be silenced. There is a sin of intolerance, but the sin of tolerance is equally dangerous. The New Testament witness reveals a narrow attitude toward doctrinal error. The writers of those sacred books realized that the result of theological misinformation could be the eternal separation of a man from his Creator. Space scientists tell us that minute error in the mathematical calculations for a moon shot can result in a total failure of the rocket to hit the moon. A slightly altered doctrine of salvation can cause a person to miss Heaven also.

Therefore, Paul exhibits a typical New Testament attitude when he says that the mouths of those teaching contrary to God's revealed Word must be stopped. The word so translated is another compound form in Greek. It is made up of *epi*, meaning *upon* and *stoma*, meaning *mouth,* giving the sense of *upon* or *over the mouth.* It could be translated by the word *muzzle.* Now Paul does not suggest to Titus that it would simply be the ideal for such vain talkers to be silenced.

---

[1]Vance Havner, *Repent or Else* (Westwood, New Jersey: Fleming H. Revell Company, 1958), p. 23.

He issues a stern command that Titus is to see that they *are* silenced. This command neither implies nor requires the use of force. Coercion is never becoming to a Christian. The method is the same one that Jude suggested (Jude 3), namely that we should earnestly contend for the faith which has been delivered unto the saints.

The whole matter is quite urgent because these deceivers are perverting whole households. As often as not they are doing this for their own personal profit, but the seriousness of the effect is not so much caused by the motives of these deceivers as by the false doctrine resulting from these motives. The perversion of pure New Testament theology has grown steadily worse. From the early Judaizers who demanded obedience to the law of Moses as a requirement for salvation and the Gnostics with their confused Christology to the contemporary rise of the cults, Satan has utilized distorted doctrinal concepts to keep people from the truth of salvation in Christ. Entire families are still confessing their sins to a priest instead of taking them to *the* priest, Jesus Christ. Through the bold proclamation of the precious truths of God, the mouths of the lions must be muzzled.

Verse 12 *One of them, their own prophet said, Cretians are always liars, evil beasts, unemployed stomachs.*

The dwellers of Crete had become notorious for their lack of morals. To demonstrate the depths to which these people had fallen, Paul quotes a native of the island. The poet quoted is Epimenides, a sixth century B.C. resident of the island. Paul also quoted from a learned philosopher at Athens· and on other occasions demonstrated a great knowledge of the literary accomplishments of the ancients. We are told that Paul received his religious training at the feet of the famous Gamaliel in Jerusalem. His knowledge of Greek literature and philosophy makes it highly probable that he also received training elsewhere, possibly from the scholars at the University of Tarsus in his hometown. Paul often used this training to open a door for a witness for Christ. In our text he quotes Epimenides as saying that *Cretians are always liars.* They are further said to be *evil beasts,* evidently a reference to their brutishness and self-centeredness. Furthermore, they are *unemployed stomachs.* The A.V. reads *slow bellies.* But for an understanding of what is actually involved, the literal Greek rendering of *unemployed stomachs* should not be overlooked. In other words, the people of Crete had no intention of working for their food. If by trickery they could secure satisfaction for their ever-expanding stomachs, they would avoid work altogether. One wonders if this disease of laziness is not contagious when he observes the general lethargy of many Christians who desire the blessings of the Lord without having to make a contribution of time and energy to the Lord's work.

Verse 13 *This witness is true. Because of this, rebuke them sharply in order that they may be healthy in the faith.*

The judgment of Epimenides on his own people appears to be harsh and unqualified. But the apostle says that the witness of the poet is exactly correct. The church is the society of twice-born men, but in its local setting there will almost always be those who will gain admittance without regeneration. To the body of Christ they are not admitted, even though to the local group they are temporarily admitted. Such was evidently the case on Crete. Some who were unconverted were deceiving others with their lies. Titus is to meet this emergency by rebuking them sharply.

Such an action is strangely alien to the tolerant attitude of most churches today. The word translated *sharply* comes from a root meaning *to cut off.* The idea is that Titus should cut them off by proclaiming truth in the power of the Holy Spirit. It must be remembered that in the Apocalypse the church at Thyatira received a stiff rebuke from the Lord of the lampstands for allowing Jezebel to teach in their Sunday school (Revelation 2:20). The power of churches would be more like it was at Pentecost and less like it was at Laodicea if churches would deal with heresy in a proper fashion.

It is not bigotry to insist on doctrinal purity. It is not an infringement upon the academic freedom of our professors in Christian institutions to release them if they violate the plain teachings of the Bible. No one thinks it is wrong to snatch the child from the path of the rattlesnake. The analogy is especially appropriate. The poison of the rattlesnake only destroys the body. The poison of falsehood destroys the soul. It is concern for lost men that should prompt us to guard the great doctrines of the Bible.

Verse 14 *Not assenting to Jewish myths and commandments of men which pervert the truth.*

Paul stresses the danger of Jewish myths and commandments of men which turn from the truth. It is the conclusion of Scripture that men as a general rule love darkness rather than light because their deeds are evil. It is not strange to find those who have turned aside from truth because Jesus said, "I am the truth," and again, "I am the light of the world." In other words, to approach truth is to come to the light. From this the natural man turns away.

It is not clear exactly what the apostle has in mind by the expression *Jewish myths*. It may be that he had reference to fanciful stories about ancestors; or he may have had in mind the misinterpretations of God's law based on Talmudic legalism, which advocated the keeping of certain Jewish laws and traditions, such as circumcision, as essential factors in salvation. In any case, these were clearly the commandments of men and not of God.

It is an object of deep concern that even among some of the relatively evangelical Christian denominations an appeal is made to some formulated creed rather than to God's Word. This is always a dangerous practice because man is basically proud. If he is allowed to formulate his own doctrine, the resulting soteriology will usually exalt what man can do to save himself. Such is the mistake of those who insist on baptismal regeneration and other similar doctrines. Man does not want to face the clear teaching of the Bible that salvation is in Christ alone and is obtained by His grace through our faith. The commandments of men inevitably attack the framework of Christianity at two vital points. The doctrine of Biblical authority and the doctrine of salvation are always affected.

Verse 15 *To the pure all things are pure, but to those who are corrupt and unbelieving nothing is clean but even their minds and moral judgments are defiled.*

Paul's next statement has been an enigma to many. There have been those who have felt that it smacks of antinomianism — the idea that since we are under grace we can live like the devil. But Paul makes it clear in Romans 6:1-2 that he takes no such position. "How shall they that are dead to sin live any longer therein?" Paul is not saying that one who is pure can do anything he wants, and it is all right just because his heart is right. To understand correctly Paul's statement, "to the pure all things are pure," it will be necessary to observe the relationships between salvation and purity. The purity about which Paul speaks is not *acquired* purity. It is *bestowed* purity. Paul says that there are none who are righteous (Romans 3:10). If our only hope is in our own righteousness or purity, then we are condemned already.

The only way we can become pure is to be purified by regeneration. David requested of God what he could not accomplish for himself when he prayed, "Wash me thoroughly from my iniquity, and cleanse me from my sin" (Psalm 51:2). Therefore, the pure about whom Paul speaks in this verse are those who are pure by virtue of the atoning sacrifice of Christ and the Holy Spirit's application of that sacrifice at the humble broken-hearted request of the sinner. Now to the one thus purified all things are pure. Although it would not be grammatically acceptable, I think it will grasp the thought of Paul to translate the phrase, "to the pure in Christ, only a pure life will be desired." Christianity is sometimes accused of a negative attitude. But this is a positive statement that regenerate men will live pure lives through the dynamic of the Holy Spirit within them.

By way of contrast, everything is turned into corruption by those who are themselves corrupt. Notice that Paul describes the first group with the one word *pure*. To Paul that required regeneration. However, the second group is given a double designation. They are *unclean* or *corrupted*, and the reason for that condition is that they are *unbelieving*. Too little emphasis has been given to that word *unbelieving*. The Greek word is *apistia*. The alpha negative is coupled with the word *pistis*, which is actually the Greek noun meaning *faith*. These corrupted individuals about whom Paul speaks are in that condition because they are without faith. When we use the verb *pisteuō*, which comes from the same root as *pistis*, we translate it *believe* because faith is only a noun in English and has no verbal equivalent.

Therefore, to believe in Christ is actually a commitment of faith on the part of a sinner. Intellectual admission will not suffice. This group of corrupted individuals on Crete had intellectually accepted the reality of God and even of Christ. But without faith, it is impossible to please God (Hebrews 11:6). This is one of Satan's most effective devices. Countless thousands are deceived this very day. They know of God but have never realized that they must know God experientially if there is to be salvation.

But the picture of these corrupt, faithless people grows darker. Paul states that even their minds and their moral judgments are completely defiled. A mind may become so oriented in its own understandings that it is blind to the tragic void created by the absence of Christ in the life. Moral judgment is then affected. Black and white have a tendency to disappear, and everything becomes gray. The condition of a man outside of Christ is serious indeed.

Verse 16 *They profess to know God, but in works deny him, being abominable and unbelieving and to every good work worthless.*

While visiting in Mississippi in a revival, I sat down by an old Negro man on the steps of a country store. I inquired his name, and he replied that it was Willie Lee. When I asked if he knew Jesus, tears began to roll down his black cheeks; and he replied pitifully that he did not know Jesus. Willie Lee's honesty was exceptional in modern America.

Many Americans are like those whom Paul describes as professing to know God verbally but denying Him in their actions. It is easy to say that we are Christians. But if our actions do not demonstrate fellowship with Christ, it provides proof that we do not really know Him. Of these professors Paul uses three descriptive terms. First, they are *abominable* as far as God is concerned. The word means *detestable*. God cannot abide their presence because they are stained with sin. In their relation to God they are unbelieving with the result of disobedience. The word *apeitheia* comes from *peithō*, meaning *to persuade usually with the result of obedience*. These whose minds and moral judgments have been defiled cannot be persuaded to obedience to Christ. Finally, with regard to life itself, unbelievers are *worthless* to all good works. This does not mean that an unbeliever never does anything good. It means that whatever good he does is worthless in God's sight unless he stands in Christ.

The necessity for healthy doctrine has been made evident in chapter one of Titus. In the last portion of this chapter Paul has carefully distinguished the believer and his manner of life from the unbeliever. Most of the last two chapters are devoted to positive exhortations for Cretian Christians.

Chapter Five

PERSONAL HOLINESS IN AN UNHOLY DAY

Titus 2:1-10

1 But you speak the things which become healthy doctrine.
2 Aged men are to be temperate, serious, self-controlled, sound in faith, love, and steadfast endurance.
3 In the same way, aged women are to behave as holy individuals, not as slanderers, neither should they be slaves to much wine, but teachers of what is good,
4 So that they might instruct the young women to be lovers of their husbands and children,
5 Serious, chaste, keepers of the home, kind, obedient to their own husbands so that the Word of God be not exposed to reproach.
6 In the same way exhort the young men to be sober-minded;
7 You yourself exhibiting right conduct concerning all things, in pure doctrine, and seriousness.
8 Using sound language, not worthy of condemnation, so that our enemies may feel ashamed, not having anything evil to say concerning us.
9 Slaves are to be obedient to their own masters in all things, pleasing them well, not contradicting them,
10 Not pilfering, but displaying all good faith so that the teachings of our Saviour God may be adorned in all things.

Verse 1 *But you speak the things which become healthy doctrine.*

Christ-like preachers are important. But, Christ-like congregations are essential. There is no double standard in the New Testament. Paul has listed the ministerial qualifications, and he now turns to individual Christianity. The instructions given by Paul are to be relayed by Titus to the local churches on Crete. Titus is therefore instructed to speak those things which become healthy doctrine. The emphasis is on the oral presentation of sound doctrine. One hears much preaching today that is neither doctrinal nor evangelistic. Most great revivals have been accompanied by great doctrinal preaching, and it is urgent that we return to this type of preaching.

Verse 2 *Aged men are to be temperate, serious, self-controlled, sound in faith, love, and steadfast endurance.*

The first instructions are for the older men of the churches. The word *presbutas* in this instance denotes the aged men of the congregation rather than the pastors. These are the natural leaders of the church, and accordingly they receive the first set of instructions. These instructions stress a holy way of life for an unholy day, and they are therefore of considerable significance in the present age.

There are six requirements specified. These may be divided into two groups of three each. The first group has to do with the ethics of an aged saint, while the last group emphasizes the spiritual walk. Morally, these aged men are to be temperate. The word *temperate* is used to denote a general practice of not overindulging in a good thing, such as eating, and of abstaining altogether from that which is hurtful, such as strong drink. Though cigarettes and other hurtful drugs were doubtless not in the apostle's mind, the basic principle nevertheless is applicable. The aged men must also be serious. This neither eliminates a sense of humor nor prohibits a happy attitude and spirit. It does mean that an aged man should be seriously committed to the work at hand. He is to be serious about Bible study and about the salvation of those outside of Christ.

In traveling overseas, I have carefully observed preachers on several occasions. Many have set a tremendous example, but a few have left much to be desired. In one instance, a popular preacher from America barked at a waitress as if she had committed the unpardonable sin, "Those eggs were not cooked enough!" The whole problem was that this man was not serious about his task in the Orient. The last moral quality listed by Paul is that of self-control. Self-control is the fine art of being able to subject oneself wholly to Spirit-control. Self-control means that one desires this Spirit-control so much that his own personal desires assume a place of relative unimportance.

Orthodoxy, attitude, and labor are also important to the aged, and these things are now presented by the apostle. Did you notice that Paul instructed the aged men to be sound in doctrine just as he demanded this quality of pastors? To be sound in doctrine necessarily implies knowing doctrine! It is not just the minister who is to be an avid student of the Bible. The aged men of the church are to study diligently the Scriptures with the intent of showing themselves approved unto God. This knowledge should be mixed with an abundance of love for Jesus and love for the lost.

A seminary professor recently said of a certain group of students, "They read everything, but accomplish almost nothing." He was not objecting to their reading or their knowledge. He was aware of the futility of knowledge for the sake of knowledge. If one loves Christ, he will keep his words; and Jesus says, "As you are going, make disciples" (Matthew 28:19). If one is knowledgeable and sound in doctrine and if he carries love deep in his inmost being, the result will be steadfast endurance in his labor. The word for *patience* is *hupomonē*. The picture is not that of meekly submitting to whatever the world imposes. Rather, one is to endure whatever obstacle Satan throws in the way and keep pressing toward the mark for the prize of the high calling of God in Christ Jesus.

The idea which Paul is advancing may be illustrated by the athlete who has run a cross-country race. The obstacles have been many. The race is almost over. He is exhausted. Yet, with his eyes affixed to the stand of the judges, he manages one last burst of speed and crosses the finish line as victor. He has patiently endured, and there is now rest from his labor and reward for his effort.

Verse 3 *In the same way, aged women are to behave as holy individuals not as slanderers, neither should they be slaves to much wine, but teachers of what is good,*

The aged are to be an example, and this is true of elderly women as well as men. These women are to be characterized by holy behavior. A woman whose general behavior is just slightly promiscuous will do great harm to the cause of Christ. Very few things in this world can be as effective a tool for Satan as a woman who verbally owns the name of Jesus but in action demonstrates unholiness. On the other hand, nothing is more impressive than a beautiful woman living a holy life for the sake of a sovereign Lord. In fact, this is what makes a woman an object of beauty.

What is meant by holiness? The term which the apostle used is a rare one in the New Testament. Its etymological foundations evidently rest on an ancient pre-Greek word for God.[1] If this is true, then it may be said that the particular emphasis of this word is that of a close relationship to God. If a woman maintains this close relationship to her Lord, she will certainly be careful not only about dress but also about her general deportment.

However, the apostle stresses certain results of this holiness. A holy woman will not be a slanderer. The passing of tales is never indicative of Christian spirit. Holy women should not be slaves to wine. Paul has obviously recognized the enslaving quality of even the mildest of strong drinks, and he warns against such enslavement. Holy women will be teachers of good. The next verses will instruct us that the object of this teaching ministry is to inspire proper living on the part of the young ladies. Also, the good things which Paul intends are mentioned in that verse.

[1]Kittel, *op. cit.*, Vol. III, pp. 221 ff.

Verses 4 and 5 *So that they might instruct the young women to be lovers of their husbands and children, Serious, chaste, keepers of the home, kind, obedient to their own husbands so that the Word of God be not exposed to reproach.*

Young women are to be taught to be in love with their husbands and children. No admonition could be more applicable to contemporary life than this one. Life has become fragmented as never before. School activities occupy increasing portions of time for our children. Wives are working. Husbands have little time at home; and what time the family has together is usually spent in silence, bowing at the feet of the howling cyclops which has become the god of the average modern household. Family loyalties are thus divided, and any sense of responsibility vanishes away like a puff of smoke. This in turn becomes a fertile field for the seeds of sin to grow into giant entangling vines which strangle spiritual sensitivities and usually end in the divorce court, the juvenile court, and, too often, even the state institution of correction. Why? That marvelous, soothing quality called love, which John tells us is essential to the very nature of God Himself, is simply not present.

If holy Christian wives would begin to love their husbands and their children, it would revolutionize the witness of the church today. When Paul says *love*, I think he means several things. Undoubtedly a certain amount of physical love is intended, but no happy marriage or strong love has ever been constructed upon such a foundation. The love Paul is talking about is seen in a broken heart over an unsaved husband. It is the tender care of a wife who is committed to caring for a God-given responsibility, her home. It is seen in a wife obedient to her husband. Love is present where the children are taught early to trust in Jesus. There are factors that create domestic tranquility.

Young women are also to be serious. This word has been discussed in verse two. In addition, they are to be chaste. Those who are currently advocating "sexual freedom" have tried to forget that this word exists. Millions have been convinced that the Playboy philosophy is correct and that chastity is a rather Puritan point of view. Well, let us not discard those humble Puritans too fast! Was it not some of these who exhibited unparalleled courage in crossing with their families to the New World in search of freedom — a freedom which is a true freedom? Have the advocates of contemporary licentiousness blazed a trail to liberty or to hell? Is venereal disease, enslavement to narcotics, alcoholism, abortion, or a ruined life due to the shame of illegitimate pregnancy the kind of freedom we desire? That is not liberty. But liberty is what Paul had in mind when he said,

"Nevertheless, I will not be brought under the power of any" (I Corinthians 6:12).

It is probably impossible to estimate the damage to young minds which is being inflicted by our five-billion dollar per year pornography business. It is an unpleasant subject to preach about and certainly a difficult one to handle gracefully, but our preachers and parents must teach our young people the biblical point of view before they are eternally ruined. The only way to deal with commercialized sex is a renewal of biblical preaching and teaching, and legal action would certainly follow.

For the married woman this chastity involves keeping herself completely for her own husband. For young women who are not married it means that they are to behave as one who has been separated unto God. It unquestionably means refraining from methods of dress or action that would easily provoke the base nature of men. And it means abstinence from ungodly premarital sexual familiarities of any sort. It also implies a general modesty and godliness which makes for true beauty and a great witness.

Three more qualities should be a part of the lives of young women. They should be *keepers of the home.* I do not believe that this economy-mad society would make any difference to Paul in what he said to these young Christian wives on Crete. There are certain conditions, more often temporary than permanent, that would make it permissible for a wife to work. But, the emphasis of Scripture is that the wife is the keeper of the home. This is a custom which should never have been altered.

Probably because of the excitement of the moment, few newly-weds could tell anyone what they said to one another in their marriage vows. But a minister should always explain those vows before the marriage ceremony. One of those vows is obedience on the part of the wife. This is no license for dictatorial conduct on the part of the husband, but it does mean a holy submissiveness to the husband's authority. All of these things are to be done by Christian wives so that the Word of God will not be exposed to reproach. If a wife is careful to discharge these Christian duties, any husband would have to be impressed with such devotion and would soon be led to Christ.

Verses 6 through 8 *In the same way exhort the young men to be soberminded; You yourself exhibiting right conduct concerning all things, in pure doctrine, and seriousness. Using sound language, not worthy of condemnation, so that our enemies may feel ashamed, not having anything evil to say concerning us.*

Young men are to be *sober-minded,* a rather all-inclusive term denoting a reserve and caution insofar as personal gratification of worldly desires is concerned. Titus is to serve as the example by showing right conduct in all things. This includes pure doctrine and an attitude of seriousness, both of which have been previously considered. Titus is to be careful about his language.

This is a very practical aspect of Christian living that is often overlooked. A story that is just a little shady, though not "really bad," would be out of the question entirely, according to Paul. A light usage of sacred vocabulary is not to be considered by Christian young men. There is a reason for such behavior, for young men must live above the accusations which unsaved men would quickly cast upon questionable conduct. In fact, Christ-like conduct will even make unbelievers ashamed, as Paul emphatically sets forth. The reason is apparent. Witnessing the life of a great Christian is like beholding one's face in a mirror. That spotless mirror shows one what he really is. An unbeliever is ashamed in a believer's presence because he is convicted of his own unrighteousness.

Verses 9 and 10 *Slaves are to be obedient to their own masters in all things, pleasing them well, not contradicting them, Not pilfering, but displaying all good faith so that the teachings of our Saviour God may be adorned in all things.*

The last exhortation for holy living is directed to slaves. The question will immediately arise: What has this to do with us? We are not slaves. First, let it be made clear that Paul does not pass approval upon slavery by dealing with the correct attitude of slaves in Titus or Philemon. He simply recognizes a situation which, though he cannot by himself abolish it, he can nevertheless make it work to the advantage of the slave, of the owner, and of God. Now how does this apply to us? To begin with, the day may be near at hand when we, like the suffering Christians of Russia, China, and Cuba, will be called upon to be the slaves of some Iron Curtain system. This indeed seems to be the condition described in the Apocalypse, chapter thirteen, during the time of the Tribulation. Christians are almost always found in slavery in some part of the world. We must be prepared to use even that slavery as a witness to the power of Christ. There is also another consideration that is even more important. As has been noted earlier, Paul often referred to himself as a bond servant of Christ. If a slave ought to conduct himself in this prescribed manner, how much greater should the dedication of the individual Christian be to his Master! Verses nine and ten should be read with this last consideration carefully in mind.

Notice that slaves are to be obedient to their own masters in all things. The only exception would be in moral or spiritual matters which concern a man's commitment to a higher authority. Slaves are to please their masters well. Can you imagine the impact of a New Testament church determined to obey the Lord completely and to please not themselves but Christ? That would shake any city! Slaves are never to contradict their masters.. They are not to pilfer or take that which does not rightfully belong to them. No amount of rationalizing will permit this. They are to display good faith so that the teachings of Jesus may be richly adorned and ornamented.

This last phrase provides a fitting conclusion for this chapter on personal holiness. The teachings of Christ may be compared to the natural beauty of a stately evergreen. The tree is full of life and vitality, standing as a picture of hope in a savage and cold environment. At Christmas someone takes that beautiful tree and adorns it with lights and other decorations, and its beauty is enhanced and made even more appealing. Godly, holy lives act as lights on that tree. They light it and reveal the inherent beauty of the teachings of Jesus Christ. No greater testimony can be given than that of a transformed, holy life.

Chapter Six

LIVING EXPECTANTLY

Titus 2:11-3:2

11 For the grace of God has been revealed in saving power to all men,

12 Teaching us that while renouncing ungodliness and worldly desires, we should live soberly, righteously, and godly in the present age,

13 Looking for the blessed hope and the revelation of the glory of our great God and Saviour, Jesus Christ,

14 Who gave himself for us in order that he might redeem us from all iniquity and cleanse for himself a special people zealous for good works.

15 Speak these things, and exhort and reprove with all authority. Let no one disregard you.

3

1 Remind them to be submissive to magistrates and to obey authorities, being prepared to undertake any good work,

2 Never reproaching anyone or being contentious, but gentle, exhibiting constant meekness before all men.

On the shelves of my library are numerous volumes on the history of this world. But each book is incomplete. The last chapter of history will be written by God Himself. Indeed, it has already been written in the form of prophecy. A part of that prophetic history is contained in the section of Titus to which we will now give our attention. This is one of two sections in the book of Titus that must be considered among the most profound of Paul's doctrinal teachings and resultant applications.

The study of eschatology has been sadly neglected by the average church member. Several factors have contributed to this neglect. The nature of the material involved, extreme attitudes on both sides, and fear have all had a hand in creating a condition of general ignorance concerning last things. The reader is urged to undertake his own biblical study of this subject. However, a word must be said here concerning interpretation. With the worsening of social conditions and an alarming theological ferment, postmillennialism has died a slow, thorough death.

Theologians now divide themselves into two main camps. Amillennialism is a system which avoids a literal interpretation in apocalyptic literature. It had its foundation with Origen (A.D. 250), who insisted that an allegorical interpretation was necessary to a correct understanding of Scripture. This system, if consistently applied, results in the exclusion of most miraculous or supernatural elements in

Scripture. These Scriptural statements are thought of as vehicles of expression rather than historic events. Most amillennialists do not carry the figurative approach this far, but its dangers are still apparent.

A much safer position is the one which requires a literal understanding of Biblical linguistics unless there is an obvious reason for a figurative interpretation. This is the general position of millenarians or, as we prefer to call them, Chiliasts.[1] While this particular theological battleground cannot be made a test of fellowship, neither should it be relegated to the place of unimportance which it now occupies. With this brief explanation of this author's position, we shall proceed to examine the present text.

Verse 11 *For the grace of God has been revealed in saving power to all men,*

Buddhism and Confucianism tell us of great men who through their own meditations became spiritually enlightened, while Greek mythology tells us of men who became gods. Only Christianity from all the religions of our world tells the unique story of God who became man, yet retained His deity. The incarnation of Christ is an essential foundational doctrine of the Christian faith, and verse eleven gives expression of that doctrine. The unmerited favor of God has been revealed in the person of Jesus Christ. In this spotless, sinless God-man, we may behold power — saving power. The heart of God is inextricably bound up in the work of human redemption.

Saving power was the subject of the first gospel announcement (Genesis 3:15). It was symbolical in the substitution of the ram for Isaac on Abraham's altar. It was the theme of the angel's song in the shepherds' fields at Bethlehem. It was the divine reason for the cross and the established foundation for final redemption to be inaugurated at the coming of Christ for His own. Saving power is revealed in Christ.

Verses 12 and 13 *Teaching us that while renouncing ungodliness and worldly desires, we should live soberly, righteously, and godly in the present age, Looking for the blessed hope and the revelation of the glory of our great God and Saviour, Jesus Christ,*

After the transformation of the new birth, this saving power which has been revealed to men begins through the Holy Spirit to teach us a new way of life. This we may call *expectant living.* I wandered into the stork club (the expectant fathers' waiting room) of a large southern hospital one day. Never have I witnessed such electric

---

[1]*Chilia* is the Greek word found in the New Testament meaning *one thousand.*

expectation or such happy rejoicing when it was announced that one father had a new son. If something of that "stork club" expectation could be infused into the lives of Christians, the world would listen to what we say!

Expectant living renounces ungodliness and worldly lusts. Our home is not this earth. We are but pilgrims, ambassadors of Christ. We must live as if the important thing were not this world but the satisfaction of our Saviour. Positively, we are to live soberly because our environment is a sobering one. We are to conduct ourselves righteously and godly in this present evil age. Sobriety reflects one's relation to himself, righteousness speaks of one's relations with his fellow man, and godliness represents one's relationship to God.

These qualities are to characterize our lives as we look for *the blessed hope,* the appearing of our Lord Jesus Christ. What is this *blessed hope?* Is it the tribulation period? What hope is found if the church must tread its way through the deep waters of tribulation with conditions evidently surpassing anything ever before experienced in human suffering? The *blessed hope* is the revelation of Jesus Christ in His glory.

He has already been revealed once in saving power. Next time He shall be revealed in His glory. When He came the first time, He was known as the Suffering Servant. But next time we shall behold Him as Supreme Sovereign. Last time He was the Carpenter of Nazareth. This time He shall be the Conqueror of the Nations. He was once made a curse for man but shall finally be the King of Kings. He formerly rode into Jerusalem on the back of an humble donkey, but the clouds of heaven will be a chariot of splendor for the King of Kings when He comes again.

The revelation of Christ in His glory is the next great event in redemptive history. The doctrines of the two revelations of Christ are inseparable. One who majors on either doctrine to the neglect of the other is not a New Testament preacher. Redemption cannot begin without the manger, cross, and empty tomb. It cannot end without the glorious return of the Lord.

Paul discusses this coming of Christ for His Church at length in I Thessalonians 4. Here, his concern is with the proper attitude toward this event. The believer should be looking for Christ. That is an active verb. He is not to be sleeping, nor is he to be tied up in the pursuit of this world. Rather, he is to be looking for Jesus. But why is this so important to Paul? Three things must be noted: (1) The coming of Christ completes the redemption of every believer. The dead in Christ are resurrected; the living in Christ are translated. Bodily redemption takes place. The rest of creation must go on travailing for a little time, but the redemption of the individual is finished! (2) The coming of Christ marks victory day. The world has scorned the lowly child of God. Lions have feasted on his flesh. Now every knee bows before the believer's Lord. (3) Above all, the coming of Christ means a face-to-face encounter with our precious Lord who loved us and bought us with His own blood. We are moved to say with John, "Even so, come, Lord Jesus!"

Verse 14 *Who gave himself for us in order that he might redeem us from all iniquity and cleanse for himself a special people zealous for good works.*

This Jesus who is to be revealed in glory has done a marvelous thing in this world. He gave Himself for us. There was a reason for this gift. He gave Himself in order that He might redeem us from all iniquity. The word *lutrōsētai,* meaning *redeem,* is significant. In the Greek New Testament this word is in the middle voice, a linguistic phenomenon which the English cannot reproduce. A. T. Robertson has pointed out the significance of the Greek middle voice. The middle voice is employed in Greek to call special attention to the subject of the verb. The subject is acting in some way which directly relates to himself.[2] Now let us apply that rule. The subject is the pronoun *who* which has as its antecedent *Jesus Christ* in verse thirteen. So it is Jesus who is the Author of our redemption. None other name is given for our salvation, only Jesus. He is essential and sufficient. But look again. It is not for our sakes alone that He redeems us, but also for the sake of having a special people who have voluntarily died to themselves in order to live to Christ. These are to be *zealous for good works.*

In addition, we are not redeemed from the eternal punishment of hell only. We are also redeemed from the strangling hold of iniquity. We need to remember that we are no longer free to indulge in iniquity. We have been freed from sin's power. This has been accomplished by a cleansing effected through the shedding of Christ's blood on the cross.

It is interesting to see the completeness of the picture of salvation which is given in these verses. We see in three verses the whole stage of redemptive history. Verse eleven says that the grace of God has been revealed in saving power. That is salvation in past time. Present tense salvation is seen in verse twelve in that we are now able to shun ungodliness and worldly lusts due to the saving power of Christ. Finally, verse thirteen reveals future salvation or the consummation of salvation, namely the revelation of Jesus in glory.

---

[2]A. T. Robertson, *A Grammar of the Greek New Testament in the Light of Historical Research* (Nashville: Broadman Press, 1934), p. 804.

Verse 15 *Speak these things, and exhort and reprove with all authority. Let no one disregard you.*

Titus is instructed to speak these things. Boldly he is to preach and teach both revelations of Christ. Once again the emphasis is upon public proclamation. John the Baptist, with nature's boulder pulpit, river baptistry, and heaven-domed sanctuary, was privileged to announce the first coming of Christ. We are doubly privileged. We proclaim the efficacy of the first coming and the surety of the second.

Paul further tells Titus to do this proclamation, exhorting and reproving with all authority. So powerful and positive is his presentation to be that even if one is not persuaded to rely on Jesus, he is not able to disregard the fervor of the message thus proclaimed.

Verse 1 *Remind them to be submissive to magistrates and to obey authorities, being prepared to undertake any good work,*

A good Christian should be a good citizen. Chapter 3 of Titus begins with a reminder of that responsibility. Obedience to those who are in authority never fails to impress men. This is a Christian virtue.

Verse 2 *Never reproaching anyone or being contentious, but gentle, exhibiting constant meekness before all men.*

The over-all attitude of an expectant Christian should not be one of gossip or of heaping reproach upon others. It is essential that we be aware of the faults of others and especially of our own. It is not necessary to call attention to such faults. Intercessory prayer is the proper way to discuss the faults of others. Nor is a Christian to be a quarrelsome individual. If our hearts are full of love and joy as we claim, contentiousness will be a difficult frame of mind to achieve. Positively, expectant believers are to be gentle and meek. Neither word pictures cowardice or weakness. On the contrary, they are descriptive of courage, commitment, strength, and resolution. Only a Christian can so master himself.

Chapter Seven

THE REASON FOR THE HOPE WHICH IS IN US

Titus 3:3-8

3 For we ourselves were once unintelligent, disobedient, deceived, being slaves to various desires and pleasures, living in wickedness and envy, despised and hating one another.

4 But when the goodness of our Saviour God and his love toward men was revealed,

5 Not out of works of righteousness which we have done but according to his mercy he saved us by the washing of regeneration and the renewing of the Holy Spirit,

6 Whom he poured out upon us richly through Jesus Christ our Saviour,

7 So that having been justified by his grace we might become heirs in fulfillment of our hope of eternal life.

8 The word is trustworthy, and concerning these counsels, I want you to affirm them strongly, in order that those who have believed in God might be careful to maintain good works. These things are worthy and profitable to men.

The resurrection of Jesus Christ is one of the greatest events of history. Its effects were numerous and astonishing. Not among the least of those effects was the transformation of a cowering, swearing fisherman named Peter into a flaming evangelist. So radical was the change that years later the apostle wrote, "Sanctify the Lord God in your hearts: and be ready always to give an answer to every man that asketh you a reason of the hope that is in you with meekness and fear" (I Peter 3:15). Any Christian who is living in eager anticipation of the appearance of Jesus will be easily marked because of his willingness to give verbal expression to the hope that is in him through Christ.

In this third chapter of Titus occurs one of the most amazing descriptions of salvation to be found in God's Word. Different areas of Scripture portray salvation from varying perspectives and in numerous ways. In Titus, chapter three, we are privileged to behold in unusual clarity the work of the Holy Spirit in the matter of salvation. The importance of this passage to the New Testament understanding of salvation can scarcely be overestimated. To understand this passage is to enable us to give a powerful witness as to the hope that is in us.

Verse 3 *For we ourselves were once unintelligent, disobedient, deceived, being slaves to various desires and pleasures, living in wickedness and envy, despised and hating one another.*

Paul begins his discussion of salvation by elucidating the predicament of every man who is not a twice-born individual. Before salvation, man is characterized by the disastrous qualities enumerated by the apostle. First, the lost man is *unintelligent*. This does not mean that his intelligence quotient is below average or that his college education was poor. However, it does mean that unless both of these factors have been transformed by a unique relationship to Christ, they are in the end worthless. To accept Jesus is not to admit ignorance, but to refuse Him is to stifle not only one's intellect but also his conscience, together with the testimonies of multiplied thousands.

A man is never really intelligent until the Holy Spirit lives in his heart to give him understanding. The reason for the label *unintelligent* in regard to the lost becomes evident upon a careful examination of the following descriptive term. The term *disobedient* (Greek *apeitheis*) has reference to *one who refuses to be persuaded*. All the evidence of the truthfulness of the Christian message, irrefutable evidence, is present. But to admit the veracity of such proof would be to submit to Christ in humble obedience. Therefore, the sinner refuses to be persuaded and consequently refuses obedience. Worse still, a man outside of Christ is deceived by Satan. This is why it is so essential that a bold proclamation of the central truths of Scripture must be continually made. The best way to combat untruth and deceit has always been a fearless exposition of what truth is.

The tragic condition of every unbeliever is observed further by Paul, who says that such a man is a slave to various desires and pleasures. One would think Paul must have certainly been looking into the heart of twentieth-century civilization; but in reality he was observing only his own century, and that should tell us something about how little men have changed in two thousand years. Life is one great race with the goal being self-satisfaction. How different from Jesus, who experienced His greatest satisfaction in providing salvation for men.

In addition Paul pictures the unbeliever as one who is characterized by hate. Unbelievers often hate one another and are thus despised even by their own kind. The word which is translated *hateful* in the A.V. is the Greek word *stugētoi*. This word shares an etymological background with the word *stux* which is used in Greek mythology as the name of a river (Styx River), by which the gods swore. Whenever one of the gods violated this oath, he was deprived of his nectar and ambrosia for one year. Consequently, the river was hated or despised by them above all else. Thus, our present word came to mean *hateful*, or *despised*. This attitude of hating and hatefulness characterizes the lives of the lost; whereas Jesus says, "By this shall all men know that you are my disciples, if you have love one for another" (John 13:35).

Verses 4 and 5 *But when the goodness of our Saviour God and his love toward men was revealed, Not out of works of righteousness which we have done but according to his mercy he saved us by the washing of regeneration and the renewing of the Holy Spirit,*

The discussion is now changed from that of our former state as sinners to that of God's work óf regeneration. Paul understood God to be the One who initiates salvation. When the goodness of God and His love for man were revealed in the person of Jesus, the redemptive plan of the ages was set in motion.

In verse five, however, it is made lucid that our salvation is not accomplished by anything that we do. Not out of the works of our own righteousness have we obtained divine favor, but by God's mercy. In verse three Paul said that unbelievers are deceived. One of the cleverest forms of devilish deceit is that of dependence upon what one does or does not do for salvation. Works of supposed righteousness, such as confession to a priest, baptism, paying of debts, kindness to one's neighbor, etc., make up an endless line of efforts at "self-saving," even though the Scripture speaks expressly to the effect that our righteousness is not enough.

We are saved by God's mercy. There is an interesting contrast in the Greek New Testament. Mercy is certainly a work of righteousness and grace; so we are saved by works of righteousness, namely the life, death, resurrection, and return of Christ. It is, of course, the propitiatory death of Christ which actually secures our redemption, but this act is not to be detached from the other important aspects of Christ's redemptive mission. Paul emphasized the word *we* in the sentence which says, ". . . not by works of righteousness which *we* have done but by *his* mercy he saved us." By adding the unnecessary Greek pronoun meaning *we*, Paul gave emphasis to the fact that salvation is impossible if predicated on what man has done. In contrast, God's mercy is sufficient. Also, the phrase *he saved* is in the aorist tense in Greek. The sense of the aorist is that of complete action. *He has saved us*, and that is complete salvation with no need for repetition.

The phrase reading *by the washing of regeneration* has constituted a theological battleground for many. An alarming number of scholars who are normally careful have seen in this phrase a reference to baptism.[1] Fortunately, many other equally competent theologians have shown why this interpretation is impossible.[2] There are three

---

[1]For example, *The Expositor's Greek Testament,* Vol. IV, and *Commentary on the Pastoral Epistles* by Patrick Fairbairn.

[2]See B. H. Carroll, *An Interpretation of the English Bible;* Kenneth S. Wuest, *The Pastoral Epistles in the Greek New Testament;* and W. E. Vine, *The Epistles to Timothy and Titus.*

factors in the verse which render the interpretation of baptism impossible. (1) This passage considers nothing which man does in response to the redemptive work of Christ, such as contrition, repentance, faith, baptism, etc. (2) Rather in this verse the divine side of salvation is definitely in view; i.e. it is salvation pictured from God's side. (3) The writer further insists that salvation is not obtained by our works of righteousness.

The fact that baptism is a work of righteousness is inescapably clear in Matthew 3:15 when Jesus replied to the reluctant Baptist, "Suffer it (Jesus' baptism at the hands of John) to be so now, for thus it becometh us to fulfill all righteousness." After this, Matthew tells us that John submitted and baptized the Master. In light of the above factors, Titus 3:5 cannot be a reference to baptism. What then is the meaning of this fascinating passage?

In Psalm 51, David speaks of a unique and thorough cleansing. "Wash me thoroughly from mine iniquity, and cleanse me from my sin . . . Wash me and I shall be whiter than snow." Surely no one will suggest that David had reference to New Testament baptism. He did expect a cleansing from sin, however! He shared that hope with Zechariah, who prophetically envisioned a glorious day when *a fountain* would be opened to the house of David *for sin and for uncleanness.* It is implicit that Zechariah saw his sins as being eradicated in some fountain. This was a true cleansing, one which the baptismal waters, though important for obedience and witness, could never effect. These Hebrews were looking to the same cleansing described in Titus 3:5. This is the cleansing of the Word of God accomplished through the shed blood of Christ on the cross and the application of that sacrifice to the life of the individual by the Holy Spirit. This explanation not only is free from conflict with the clear teachings of the New Testament but also is actually in wonderful harmony with them.

Ephesians 5:25-27 says, "Husbands, love your wives, even as Christ also loved the church and gave himself for it, that he might sanctify and cleanse it by the washing of water by the word, that he might present it to himself a glorious church, not having spot or wrinkle, or any such thing; but that it should be holy and without blemish." All of this is accomplished by the cleansing power of the Word. This is the same washing as that mentioned by Paul in Titus.

In that last, amazing, wonderful book of Revelation, John the apostle is exiled on Patmos. In the process of the visions which God gave to him, he saw a multitude of men clothed in white, praising the glorified Christ. One of the twenty-four elders asked John who these people were. John replied that it would probably be better for the elder to give the explanations, and he would just listen. The elder proceeded with the identification. "These are they which came out of the great tribulation and have washed their robes, and made them white in the blood of the lamb" (Revelation 7:14).

Here as throughout the New Testament we are told that all cleansing takes place in the blood of Jesus Christ which does cleanse us from all sin (I John 1:9). Titus 3:5 is talking about the application of the atonement of Christ to the heart of the sinner by the Holy Spirit. Finally, the best texts of Revelation 22:14 read, "Blessed are they that wash their robes that they may have the right to come to the tree of life, and may enter in by the gates into the city." All of this washing — and it is every bit done in the blood of the Word of God. This is the only method given for cleansing and salvation. Jesus is certainly the way, the truth, and the life!

If there is still doubt, the reader is urged to consult James 1:18 and I Peter 1:23, where references are made to the believer who is said to have been begotten by the Word of God. The simple and best conclusion is that Paul's statement in Titus 3:5 has reference to the application of Christ's blood by the Holy Spirit.

It remains for us to consider briefly the actual work of the Holy Spirit in salvation. The word *regeneration* is a combination in Greek of two words, *palin,* meaning *again,* and *ginomai,* meaning *to become.* Thus *regeneration* is *to become again* or *to have a new birth.* Now, John 3:5 tells us that this new birth is the work of the Holy Spirit. This is a once and for all happening which occurs whenever a man repents and commits himself to Christ. The Holy Spirit immediately moves into the soul of that man and applies the rich fountain of the blood of Christ. The result is *regeneration* or *a new life hid with Christ in God.*

But salvation is not finished at this point. The Holy Spirit remains in the regenerate one's heart for the day-by-day task of renewal. The word is *anakainōseōs,* a compound of the Greek preposition *ana,* meaning *again,* and *kainos,* meaning *new.* Thus, the believer is *one who is again new* or *re-newed* every day. This renewal means that the spirit of God gives new life every day until Christ comes for his own.

Verse 6 *Whom he poured out upon us richly through Jesus Christ our Saviour,*

This ministry of the Holy Spirit is pictured in verse six as having been poured out by God through Jesus Christ. The pouring hints at the abundance of this gift, and the word *richly* indicates something of the quality of the gift. This regenerating work of the Holy Spirit is wholly sufficient. Our works of righteousness, which are so very lacking, are not required for our salvation.

Verse 7 *So that having been justified by his grace we might become heirs in fulfillment of our hope of eternal life.*

The sinner's original predicament has been presented in verse three. Verses four through six have described the matchless work of God for the sinner's salvation. The result is a new condition portrayed in verse seven. The sinner is now justified or declared righteous. Once again the Greek aorist tense is employed, meaning that justification is complete. If there were nothing else in this verse, we could praise our Saviour's name for this eternal justification. Christ has paid the penalty of sin. Therefore God says that we who are His children by adoption are justified, declared righteous, because we have exchanged garments with Christ. He took our dirty, sinful garment. We took His beautiful, clean, righteous garment.

But the end is not yet. In fulfillment of our eternal hope, God has made us heirs with Christ. That is simply incredible were it not for the grace of God as evidenced on the cross. This means the glories of heaven for the Christian. It means a day of victory. It means living and reigning with Christ on this very earth. What mortal could fail to be moved in his inmost soul by comparing the sinner of verse three to the saint of verse seven? Never shall we fathom the depths of God's love and grace.

Verse 8 *The word is trustworthy, and concerning these counsels, I want you to affirm them strongly, in order that those who have believed in God might be careful to maintain good works. These things are worthy and profitable to men.*

Paul affirms that the things which he has just written are entirely *trustworthy.* Titus is therefore to speak of them with boldness. He is to do this for the benefit of the saints, who, realizing the dramatic transformation wrought by Christ, will *be careful to maintain good works.*

The word *trustworthy (pistos)* comes from the same root as the word *episteuthēn,* which occurs early in chapter one, as Paul spoke of being *entrusted* with the gospel. It is also the same root from which the Greek word *pistis,* meaning *faith,* is derived. These references help us to understand that faith is trust and commitment. Therefore, because the *Word,* which Paul has recorded under the inspiration of the Holy Spirit, is worthy of faith and trust, Titus then is adjured to affirm this *Word* strongly. The doctrines of this letter are to be emphasized regularly through a forceful and demanding presentation of the essential truths of the Gospel. For if the Gospel will indeed revolutionize man, as is its claim, surely it should be presented with a zeal of holy anticipation. The immoral populace of Crete, together with its parallel in our modern paganistic society, was in dire need of the demonstration of a Spirit-directed life through works of righteousness and holiness. Even as Paul realized that a witness supported by a genuinely transformed life would mean much to the people of Crete, so the words of Titus 3:3-8 should be incentive enough for any Christian to live for Christ.

Chapter Eight

LOVING IN THE FAITH

Titus 3:9-15

9 But avoid foolish debates and genealogies and quarrels and disputes pertaining to the law, for they are unprofitable and fruitless.

10 After a first and a second warning, reject a man who is causing divisions,

11 Knowing that such a man has been perverted and is sinning, being self-condemned.

12 When I send Artemis or Tychicus to you, lose no time coming to me at Nicopolis, for I have decided to spend the winter there.

13 Help Zenas the lawyer and Apollos on their journey with special care so that they may be deficient in nothing.

14 And let our people learn to practice diligently good works for the supply of their necessities so that they may not be unfruitful.

15 Everyone with me sends you greetings. Greet the believers who love us. Grace be with you all.

The last section of Paul's letter to Titus deals with general instructions and then contains a customary Pauline greeting. The instructions concern primarily the treatment of divisive characters within the church.

Verse 9 *But avoid foolish debates and genealogies and quarrels and disputes pertaining to the law, for they are unprofitable and fruitless.*

The early church was frequently harassed by the Judaizers. These people were strict Jewish legalists who claimed to be Christians. However, they demanded of all other Christians strict adherence to the letter of the Mosaic law. For Gentiles, this meant circumcision. For Jews it meant continued slavery to the law, which was never meant to be more than a school teacher to teach them their inadequacies. Paul would probably never have been so infuriated about the Judaizers had it not been for the nature of their teachings. Two vital subjects were affected by this doctrine: (1) The words of Jesus were contradicted. This we may call contradicting the Word of God. (2) They tampered with God's plan of salvation when additions were made to the requirements for salvation. It must be obvious that perverted doctrine invariably crosses these two areas of religion. And, of all the areas of our religious life, these two things must remain constant. Paul realized this, and therefore his language concerning these legalists is often quite strong.

51

Characteristic of these legalizers was their affinity for theological argumentation. They were interested in controversy but adamant about conversions. Theology was close to their hearts, but God was vague and far away. They knew about God but did not know Him personally in Jesus. Paul desires Titus to avoid foolish debates fostered by these Judaizers. Time is too short and too valuable to spend in philosophical theorizing. Besides, those debaters were bringing no profit to anyone and were totally void of fruit.

The application of this passage to the contemporary scene may be painful but is nevertheless essential. Christian schools and seminaries are involved increasingly in theological debate. A steady procession of theological straw men have paraded across the stage, beginning with the Old Liberalism and progressing to the quest for the Jesus of history, existentialism, neo-orthodoxy, and finally the death of God controversy.

Many other movements are even now on the wings of the stage preparing for their assault on Biblical Christianity. We are not to be surprised. Paul and Peter said that it would be this way in the last days (II Timothy 4:1-4 and II Peter 3:1-5). However, the fact that this fails to surprise the Christian should not prevent him from taking action. The church should avoid such theological debates because they are foolish, profitless, and fruitless. Those three reasons should be sufficient to lead believers to purge their churches and their church-related institutions of elements which pervert the Gospel.

This does not mean that we egotistically turn our backs on knowledge and truth from any source. Our minds must be open to new truth, and any action we take must have love as its foundation. Nevertheless, if we heed the instructions of Paul to Titus, it will necessitate a purging of those who do not accept the authority and theological inerrancy of Scripture, and of those who mutilate God's redemptive plan. This is not "heretic-hunting"; it is just plain common sense with a biblical precedent already established!

Notice carefully the two words used by Paul to describe these foolish debates. They are *profitless.* In other words, they never result in spiritual growth. They are *fruitless,* meaning that few, if any, come to Christ as a result of these debates. That these two terms describe plainly the current theological condition in many of our schools and churches is painfully clear. It must be said, however, that we thank God for many godly preachers and professors who still love the Lord and His Word. These are to be commended and encouraged. They make a contribution to the Lord's kingdom worthy of heaven's praises.

Verse 10 *After a first and a second warning, reject a man who is causing divisions,*

After a man who causes divisions in the church has been warned twice, he should be rejected, according to Paul. This must be carefully done, and that in the proper spirit. But the church suffers lack of vitality and power today partially because of its failure to exercise discipline. One who causes divisions with his doctrine or attitude will disrupt fellowship and slow down the ministry of the church. Such men have been perverted by Satan and are in the very process of sinning. Thus they are bringing condemnation upon themselves.

Verses 12 and 13 *When I send Artemis or Tychicus to you, lose no time coming to me at Nicopolis, for I have decided to spend the winter there. Help Zenas the lawyer and Apollos on their journey with special care so that they may be deficient in nothing.*

Beginning with verse twelve, we get a brief look at early missionary organization and activity. Paul is going to spend the winter at Nicopolis, and he wished to be able to spend it with his beloved Titus. The purpose of this winter retreat was probably that of planning strategy for advance. Accordingly, Paul was sending either Artemis or Tychicus to replace Titus on Crete. These were serving as apostolic delegates and advisors but probably not as pastors. Paul probably sensed that this might be his last meeting with Titus on this earth. He desired to fellowship, plan, and pray with him one last time.

Zenas, a lawyer who had possibly turned preacher, and Apollos were evidently on Crete, having been sent, perhaps as experts in Jewish matters, to deal with the Judaizers. In any case, while the revival was in progress, Titus was urged to see that the churches properly cared for the evangelistic team. They were to have need of nothing.

Verse 14 *And let our people learn to practice diligently good works for the supply of their necessities so that they may not be unfruitful.*

The people of the church were to practice diligently good works. In this situation the word *works* probably has reference to an occupation. Christians, if able at all, are always urged to work to support themselves and provide for their own needs. Christian beggars would have little witness. If anyone were in poverty, it was the responsibility of the church to care for them. Modern churches have sadly neglected this area of their ministry.

Verse 15 *Everyone with me sends you greetings. Greet the believers who love us. Grace be with you all.*

The letter is brought to a conclusion with the customary greetings.

The believers who love Paul are to be greeted. It is altogether proper that an epistle dealing with the mounting problems of an infant church should end in love.

CONCLUSION

We have already suggested that the Epistle to Titus serves as an excellent guidebook for Christian living. Its value seems to be that in a very short space it gives careful attention to redemption, eschatology, and Christian living. Such a broad scope gives to every believer a compact treatment of the great doctrines of the Christian faith. Armed with such knowledge, he is ready to witness for Jesus by the life that he lives and the message that he shares.

BIBLIOGRAPHY

Arndt, William F., and F. Wilbur Gingrich, *A Greek-English Lexicon of the New Testament and Other Early Christian Literature.* Chicago: University of Chicago Press, 1960.

Barclay, William, *The Letters to Timothy, Titus, and Philemon.* Philadelphia: Westminster Press, 1960.

Barochman, Paul F., *Proclaiming the New Testament,* Vol. VI. Grand Rapids: Baker Book House, 1964.

Barrett, C. K., *The Pastoral Epistles.* Oxford: Clarendon Press, 1963.

Baxter, J. Sidlow, *Explore the Book.* Grand Rapids: Zondervan Publishing House, 1962.

Bernard, J. H., "The Pastoral Epistles," *Cambridge Greek Testament for Schools and Colleges.* Cambridge: University Press, 1906.

Carroll, B. H., *An Interpretation of the English Bible,* Vol. XVI. Nashville: Broadman Press, 1947.

Clarke, Adam, *Clarke's Commentary,* Vol. III. New York: Abingdon Press, n.d.

Dana, H. E., and Julius R. Mantey, *A Manual Grammar of the Greek New Testament.* New York: The MacMillan Company, 1960.

Fairbairn, Patrick, *Commentary on the Pastoral Epistles.* Grand Rapids: Zondervan Publishing House, 1956.

Harrison, P. N., *The Problem of the Pastorals.* Oxford: University Press, 1921.

Havner, Vance, *Repent or Else.* Westwood, New Jersey: Fleming H. Revell Company, 1958.

Hendriksen, William, "Exposition of the Pastoral Epistles," *New Testament Commentary.* Grand Rapids: Baker Book House, 1957.

Hovey, Alvah, ed., *An American Commentary on the New Testament,* Vol. V. Philadelphia: The American Baptist Publication Society, 1890.

Ironside, H. A., *In the Heavenlies.* New York: Loizeaux Brothers, Inc., 1957.
............, *Studies in the Epistle to the Hebrews and the Epistle to Titus.* New York: Loizeaux Brothers, Inc., 1963.

Kittel, Gerhard, ed., *Theological Dictionary of the New Testament,* Vols. I, II, and III. Grand Rapids: Wm. B. Eerdmans Publishing Company, 1965.

Lock, Walter, "The Pastoral Epistles," *The International Critical Commentary.* Edinburgh: T. & T. Clark, 1936.

Nicoll, W. Robertson, ed., *Expositor's Greek Testament,* Vol. IV. Grand Rapids: Wm. B. Eerdmans Publishing Company, 1951.

Pfeiffer, Charles F., ed., *The Biblical World*. Grand Rapids: Baker Book House, 1966.

Robertson, A. T., *A Grammar of the Greek New Testament in Light of Historical Research*. Nashville: Broadman Press, 1934.

Rose, J. R., *A Handbook of Greek Mythology*. New York: E. P. Dutton & Company, Inc., n.d.

Scott, E. F., "The Pastoral Epistles," *Moffatt New Testament Commentary*. London: Hodder and Stoughton, 1948.

Shepherd, J. W., *The Life and Letters of St. Paul*. Grand Rapids: Wm. B. Eerdmans Publishing Company, 1956.

Simpson, E. K., *The Pastoral Epistles*. London: The Tyndale Press, 1954.

Spence, H. D. M., and Joseph S. Exell, eds., *Pulpit Commentary*, Vol. XXI. Grand Rapids: Wm. B. Eerdmans Publishing Company, n.d.

Stalker, James, *The Life of St. Paul*. New York: Fleming H. Revell Company, 1950.

Tenney, Merrill C., *New Testament Survey*. Grand Rapids: Wm. B. Eerdmans Publishing Company, 1962.

............, *New Testament Times*. Grand Rapids: Wm. B. Eerdmans Publishing Company, 1965.

Thayer, Joseph Henry, *A Greek-English Lexicon of the New Testament*. New York: American Book Company, 1889.

Thiessen, Henry Clarence, *Introduction to the New Testament*. Grand Rapids: Wm. B. Eerdmans Publishing Company, 1952.

Trench, Richard Chenevix, *Synonyms of the New Testament*. Grand Rapids: Wm. B. Eerdmans Publishing Company, 1947.

Unger, Merrill F., *Unger's Bible Handbook*. Chicago: Moody Press, 1966.

Vine, W. E., *The Epistles to Timothy and Titus*. Grand Rapids: Zondervan Publishing House, 1965.

Williams, Charles B., *A Commentary on the Pauline Epistles*. Chicago: Moody Press, 1953.

Wuest, Kenneth S., *Studies in the Vocabulary of the Greek New Testament*. Grand Rapids: Wm. B. Eerdmans Publishing Company, 1962.

............, *The Pastoral Epistles in the Greek New Testament*. Grand Rapids: Wm. B. Eerdmans Publishing Company, 1960.